WIND AND SUN

One day Wind was bragging
to Sun.

"I'm much stronger than you!"
Wind said.

"I can blow down chimneys.

I can blow down trees.

2

And I can blow hats off – look!"
Wind blew off the hat of a man
walking up a big hill.

4

"Okay, Wind," said Sun.
"Let's see who is stronger.
Let's see which of us can
get the man's coat off."
So Wind took a long,
deep breath, and...

6

Wind blew a gale!
All the trees bent.
All the leaves flew into the air.
All the clouds raced
across the sky.

8

When Wind blew,
the man felt so cold!
He buttoned up his coat.
He tied up his belt.
Wind just couldn't blow off
the man's coat.

10

"Now it's my turn," said Sun.

Sun shone down his warm rays.

Soon the man felt hot.

He untied his belt.

He undid the buttons, and...

12

he took off his coat.
Sun beamed a big smile,
and Wind scowled and frowned.

14

"You see," said Sun,
"Sun is stronger than Wind!"
16

The FROG PRINCESS

Long ago, there lived three princes.
One day, their father gave them
a bow and arrow.
"Shoot this arrow into the sky,"
he said. "The lady who brings
it back will be your wife."

3

The first prince shot the arrow.

Swish!

Back came a pretty princess.

The second prince shot the arrow.
Swish!
Back came a dainty duchess.

The third prince shot the arrow.
Swish!
Back came a little frog.
"I won't marry her!"
said the prince.

"Yes, you will,"
said his father.

7

So there was a grand wedding.
But the third prince was not
very happy.

The prince carried the frog princess
to royal meetings on a beautiful
green cushion.

A special pond was made
at the palace.
The prince and the frog princess
went swimming.
They became good friends.

One day, the frog princess
disappeared.
Everyone looked for her,
but she was gone.

The third prince was very sad.
"I really loved her!" he cried.
Then, SWISH...

Before him stood a beautiful princes

"Who are you?"
asked the prince.

"It's me, the little frog!"
replied the princess.
"You have broken
the spell."

So the third prince and the
princess lived happily ever after.
And never ever again did the
little frog princess wear green!